WHAT'S THE WEATHER OUTSIDE?

By CODY MCKINNEY

Illustrated by ANNIE WILKINSON

CANTATA
LEARNING

MANKATO, MINNESOTA

CANTATA
LEARNING
MANKATO, MINNESOTA

Published by Cantata Learning
1710 Roe Crest Drive
North Mankato, MN 56003
www.cantatalearning.com

Library of Congress Control Number: 2014938316
ISBN: 978-1-63290-078-4

What's the Weather Outside? by Cody McKinney
Illustrated by Annie Wilkinson

Book design by Tim Palin Creative
Music produced by Wes Schuck
Audio recorded, mixed, and mastered at Two Fish Studios, Mankato, MN

Printed in the United States of America.

3 1561 00266 1019

 VISIT

WWW.CANTATALEARNING.COM/ACCESS-OUR-MUSIC

Weather is an important part of our daily lives. It affects how and where we live, as well as what we do, eat, and wear. Weather varies in different parts of the world and at different times of year. We can often **predict** what the weather will be like. What do you like to do in different weather?

It's Saturday, and I want to play
outside. I hope that the weather is nice.
I hope all the water didn't turn to ice!

What's the **temperature**? Then
I'll know for sure what to wear.
Precipitation's up in the air,
which means it's not too dry.

Right now, the weather is cold. But in the North and South Pole, it's freezing all year long.

11

The weatherman predicts it'll stay pretty dry. But there are clouds in the sky that make it rain and snow and fog.

Outside, I start to feel the breeze on my face. It's kind of like I'm running a race. And it makes me so much colder.

I lie on the ground, watching all
the clouds up above. One looks
like a sheep, the other a dove.
But now they're moving faster.

I see a storm blowing in. It's about to begin to just sleet like crazy. Maybe later I'll move to the **equator**, where it's warm all the time and the animals have nice fur.

In the winter, the plants should
get the heat, where they stay
on the ground until it all blows
over. In the summer, the wind is
not a bummer. It keeps my body
cool when I'm off to slumber.

GLOSSARY

equator—an imaginary line that divides the earth in two halves

precipitation—water that falls to the earth in the forms of hail, mist, rain, sleet, and snow

predict—to guess or say in advance

temperature—how warm or cold it is as shown on a thermometer; a thermometer measures temperature.

weather—the precipitation, temperature, and windiness

What's the Weather Outside?

Cody McKinney

Pop Rock

Piano

It's Sa – tur – day and I wan-na play out – side. I hope that the wea-ther is

nice, I hope all the wa-ter di – dn't turn to ice..............

It's Sa – tur – day and I wan -na play out – side. I hope that the wea-ther is

nice, I hope all the wa-ter di – dn't turn to ice..............

Online music access and CDs available at www.cantatalearning.com

23

ACTIVITY

1. What is the weather like where you live? Does it change during the seasons? How?

2. What is your favorite kind of weather, and why? What is your least favorite kind of weather, and why?

3. If you lived somewhere very cold, how would the weather affect your lifestyle? What about if you lived somewhere very hot?

TO LEARN MORE

Edison, Erin. *Lightning*. Minneapolis, MN: Capstone Press, 2012.

Edison, Erin. *Snow*. Minneapolis, MN: Capstone Press, 2012.

Chanko, Pamela, and Daniel Moreton. *Weather*. New York: Scholastic, 1998.

Dussling, Jennifer, and Heidi Petach. *Pink Snow and Other Weird Weather*. New York: Grosset & Dunlap, 1998.